D0398514

TRUE OR FALSE

Planets

By MELVIN AND GILDA BERGER

Text copyright © 2010 by Melvin and Gilda Berger

ISBN 978-0-545-20204-6

10 9 8 7 6 5 4 3 2 1   10 11 12 13 14

Printed in the U.S.A.   40
First printing, September 2010
Original book design by Nancy Sabato
Composition by Kay Petronio

Planets are the same as stars.

TRUE OR FALSE?

FALSE! Planets may look like stars in the sky, but they are very different.

Stars are huge balls of hot, glowing gas that create their own light. Planets are big, dark bodies that move around stars. They do not create their own light — planets shine with the light they reflect from nearby stars. Even though planets are big, stars are much larger than planets.

The Sun is the near[ ] Star to planet Ear[ ]

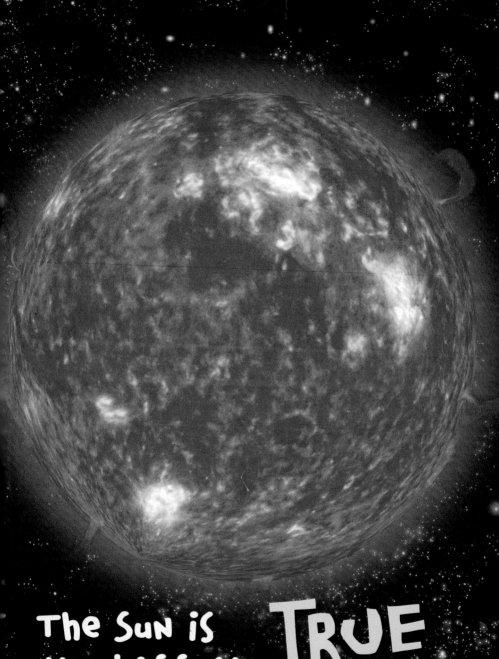

The Sun is the biggest star. TRUE OR FALSE?

FALSE! The largest known star is VY Canis Majoris.

The Sun just looks like the biggest star because it is the closest star to Earth. The Sun is close enough for us to feel its heat and see its bright light. Other stars are trillions and trillions of miles away. We cannot feel their heat. Most distant stars can be seen only with a telescope.

The Sun's volume is more than a million times larger than that of Earth.

The planets and the Sun make up our entire Solar System.

TRUE OR FALSE?

FALSE!

The Solar System includes not just eight planets and the Sun, but also moons, comets, asteroids, and dwarf planets.

The Sun is at the center. The eight planets — Mercury, Venus, Earth, Mars, Jupiter, Saturn, Uranus, and Neptune — move, or revolve, in paths around the Sun. These paths are called orbits. The planets revolve around the Sun at different speeds.

The time a planet takes to complete orbit is one year c that planet.

The
planets
spin as
they orbit
the Sun.

TRUE
OR
FALSE?

TRUE! Each planet spins as it goes around the Sun.

No two planets spin, or rotate, at the same speed. As each planet rotates, the Sun shines on different parts of the planet. It is daytime in the part lit by the Sun. It is nighttime in the part without sunlight.

The time it takes planet to make a f rotation is one day that planet.

Astronauts weigh the same on Earth as they would on other planets.

TRUE OR FALSE?

FALSE!

An astronaut's weight would be different on each planet. It all depends on the pull of gravity. Gravity on the huge planet Jupiter is stronger than on any other planet. An astronaut who weighs 150 pounds (68 kilograms) on Earth would weigh 355 pounds (161 kilograms) on Jupiter. Mercury is much, much smaller than Jupiter. Its gravity is far weaker. The same astronaut would weigh only 57 pounds (26 kilograms) on Mercury.

The Sun's gravity keeps the planets their orbits.

All planets are made of rock and metal.

TRUE OR FALSE?

TRUE! All planets are made of rock and metal; some are also gas and liquid.

The four planets closest to the Sun — Mercury, Venus, Earth, and Mars — are all similar. They are made of rock and metal. But the four planets farthest from the Sun — Jupiter, Saturn, Uranus, and Neptune — are different. Their solid cores are surrounded by huge layers of gas and liquid.

The four planet
farthest from t
Sun are called th
gas giants.

Jupiter

Saturn

Uranus

Nept

Sun

Mercury

Venus

Earth / Moon

Mars

Mercury is
the planet
closest to
the Sun.

TRUE
OR
FALSE?

TRUE! Mercury is the closest planet to the Sun.

It is also the smallest of all the planets and has the shortest orbit. The Sun is so close that its powerful rays make Mercury one of the brightest planets. Look carefully to see Mercury low in the sky just after sunset or before dawn. From Earth, Mercury looks like a distant star.

Due to its shorter orbit, a year on Mercu lasts only eighty-eigh Earth days!

The Surface
of Mercury
is covered
with holes.

TRUE
OR
FALSE?

TRUE!

Big and Small holes cover Mercury.

Over billions of years, large numbers of meteoroids and comets have crashed into Mercury. They created deep holes, called craters, in the planet's surface. In 1974, a spacecraft, *Mariner 10*, flew within 437 miles (703 kilometers) of Mercury. Photos taken by *Mariner 10* give close-up views of the craters.

Mercury's largest crater is about 800 mile (1,300 kilometers) across about the distance from N York City to Chicago.

Venus is the hottest planet in the solar system.

TRUE OR FALSE?

TRUE! Venus is the hottest planet

because it's close to the Sun and also wrapped in thick clouds. The heat from the Sun passes through the clouds and warms the planet's dry, rocky surface. Then the clouds work like blankets. They hold in the heat and do not let it escape. This traps the Sun's powerful heat on Venus's surface and makes the planet very hot.

The air on Ven is mostly carb dioxide.

The Surface of Earth is mostly land.

TRUE OR FALSE?

FALSE! The Surface of Earth has much more water than land.

In fact, 70.8 percent of Earth's surface is covered in water. From space, Earth looks like a giant ball of blue with a few other colors. The blue is Earth's oceans. The white is the clouds above Earth, or parts of the surface that are covered with ice. The brown or green that shows through the clouds is rocks, soil, and plants.

The oceans hold 97 percent of the water on Earth.

Earth is the only planet with one moon.

TRUE OR FALSE?

TRUE! None of the other planets has one single moon.

The other planets have anywhere from zero to more than sixty moons. Each moon is a ball of rock that orbits the planet. Moons are always smaller than the planets they travel around. Just like planets, the moons reflect the light they get from the Sun.

Earth's moon circle the planet once eve twenty-nine days.

Earth's moon is a windy place.

TRUE
OR
FALSE?

FALSE! Earth's moon has no wind or other weather.

On July 20, 1969, Neil Armstrong became the first person to walk on the Moon. Over the years, eleven other astronauts followed. They did not find any signs of weather on its surface — and Neil Armstrong's footprints were still there. Without wind or rain, the footsteps the astronauts left behind may be there forever.

Earth's moon is our closest neighbor in spa

Mars is called the Red Planet.

TRUE OR FALSE?

TRUE! Mars is called the Red Planet because its surface is reddish orange in color.

The rocks and soil on Mars contain iron. Long ago there was water on Mars. The water rusted the iron and turned it red. Strong winds blow the red soil up into the sky.

Mars is about ha the size of Eart

Astronauts
have landed
on Mars.

TRUE
OR
FALSE?

FALSE! No astronaut has ever visited Mars — or any other planet.

But scientists do send robotic spacecraft, without astronauts, into orbit around Mars. Sometimes the scientists send robots to the surface of Mars. The robots take photos; collect samples of soil, rocks, and gases; and measure conditions on the planet.

The North and Sou~ poles of Mars are covered with ice

Jupiter is the largest planet in the Solar System.

TRUE OR FALSE?

TRUE!

Jupiter is so big, more than 1,000 Earths could fit inside it. Jupiter is more than eleven times the size of Earth. Jupiter is also the heaviest planet. Because of its great size, ancient astronomers named Jupiter after the king of the Roman gods.

EARTH

JUPITER

The second-large planet in the Sola System is Saturn

The Great
Red Spot is a
gigantic storm
on Jupiter.

TRUE
OR
FALSE?

TRUE! Jupiter's Great Red Spot is the most violent storm in the solar system.

Astronomers are not sure what causes the Great Red Spot or where it gets its color. Over the years, the color of the Great Red Spot has ranged from brick red to almost white. In the last few years, the Great Red Spot has been shrinking.

The Great Red Spot is at least 300 years old.

Saturn is the only planet with rings.

TRUE OR FALSE?

FALSE! Jupiter, uranus, and Neptune also have rings.

But Saturn's rings are brighter than those of the other planets. Saturn is surrounded by thousands of thin, flat rings. The rings are made up of billions of pieces of ice, rock, and dust. Each piece is like a tiny mirror that shines because it bounces back the Sun's light.

The first astronomer to see Saturn's rings thought that the planet had "handles."

Saturn always looks the same from Earth.

TRUE OR FALSE?

FALSE! Our view of Saturn keeps changing.

For half of its travels around the Sun, the top of Saturn is pointing toward us. We see Saturn's rings from above. For the other half of its journey, the top of Saturn is pointing away from us. We see the rings from below. When Saturn is tilted sideways, the rings almost disappear.

It takes almost thirty Earth yea for Saturn to or the Sun once.

uranus spins
like all the
other planets. TRUE
OR
FALSE?

FALSE! Uranus is the only planet that does not spin like a top.

Uranus is tilted on its side. It rolls around like a barrel, not a top. For half its orbit, Uranus's north pole points toward the Sun and the south pole points away. For the rest of the time, the south pole points toward the Sun and the north pole points away.

Each half of Uranus is light for forty-two years and dark for forty-two years.

Neptune is the stormiest planet.

TRUE OR FALSE?

TRUE!

winds blow around Neptune about three times faster than the strongest hurricanes on Earth. An especially fierce, violent storm was discovered in 1989 and named the Great Dark Spot. But by 1991, it had mysteriously vanished. Since then, a similar dark spot has been discovered in Neptune's northern hemisphere.

Neptune's largest moon, Triton, is th coldest known obje in the solar system

Pluto is a planet.

TRUE OR FALSE?

FALSE! Pluto is no longer considered a planet.

In 2006, astronomers decided that Pluto was a dwarf planet, not a true planet, because of its size and place in the solar system. Pluto is far, far smaller than any of the planets — less than one-fifth the size of Earth. It is also at the outer edge of the solar system — almost forty times farther away from the Sun than Earth is.

There are fiv
dwarf planets
our Solar Syste

There are no planets beyond the Solar System.

TRUE

OR

FALSE?

FALSE!

There are about 400 known planets outside our Solar System. And every year astronomers keep finding more. They call these planets extrasolar planets. Extrasolar planets orbit distant stars. With potentially hundreds of billions of planets in space, the future is exciting indeed!

Most of the extrasolar planets found so far are gas giants like Jupiter.

Index